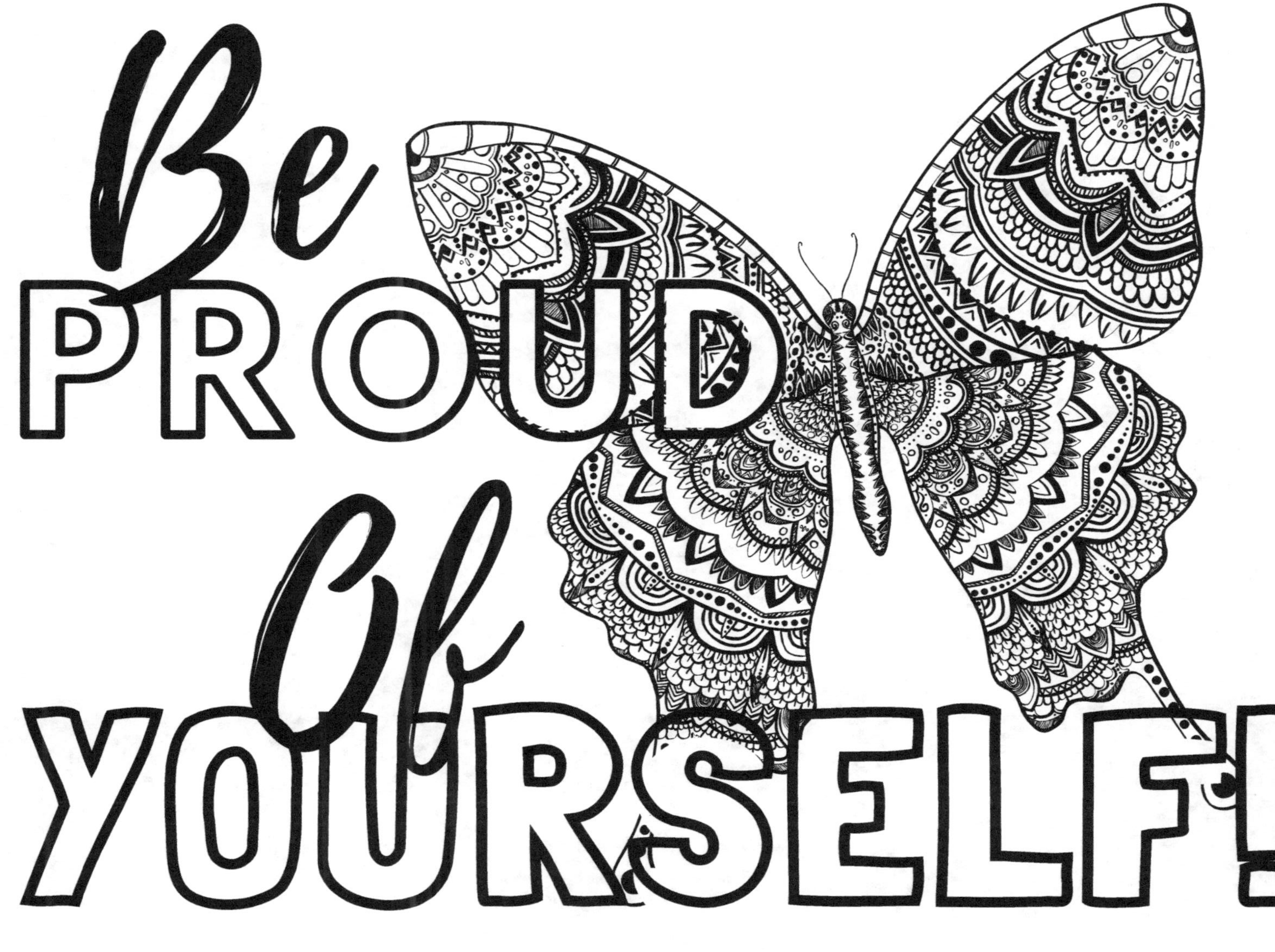

Add Your Personal Doodles

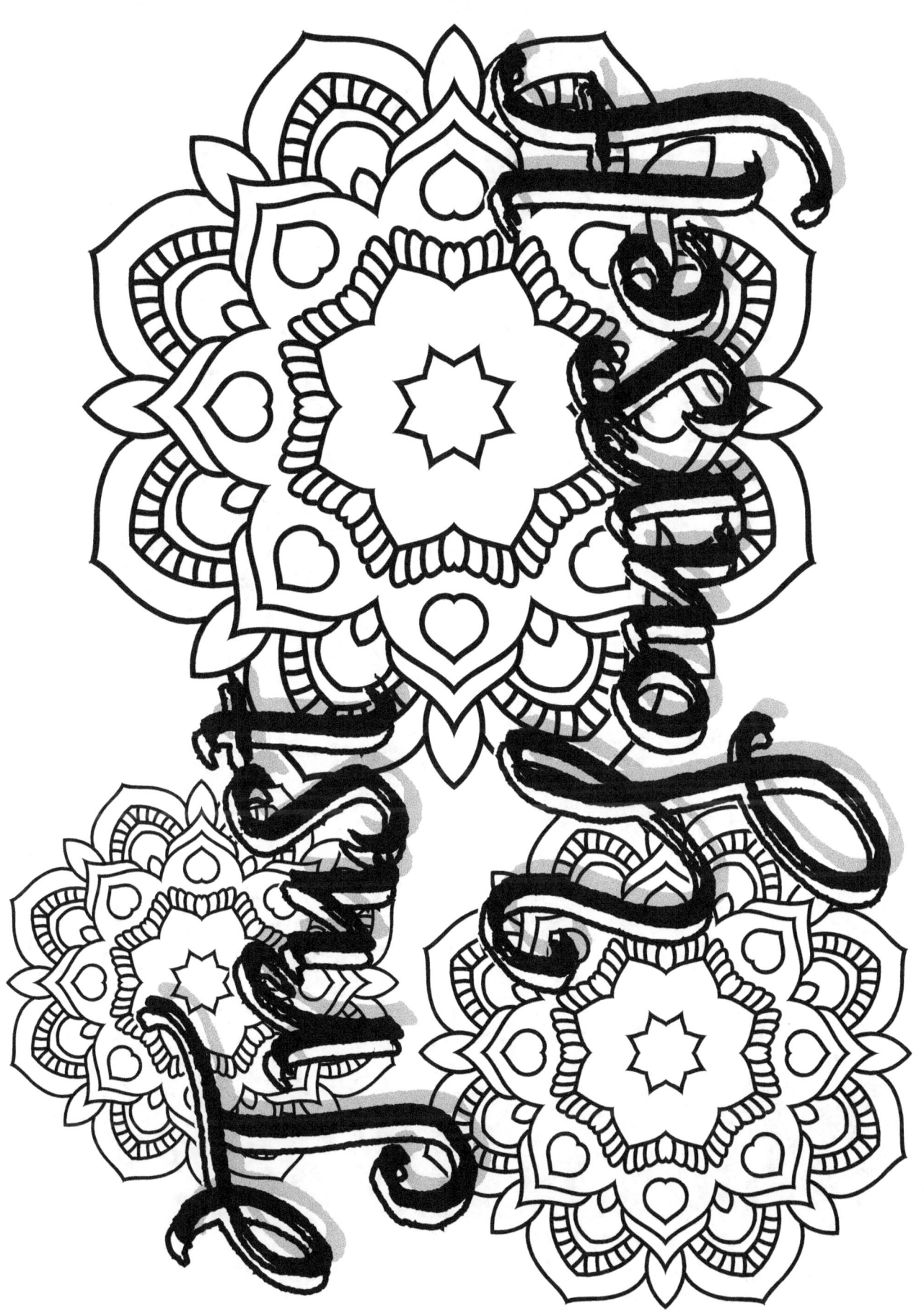

Add Your Personal Doodles

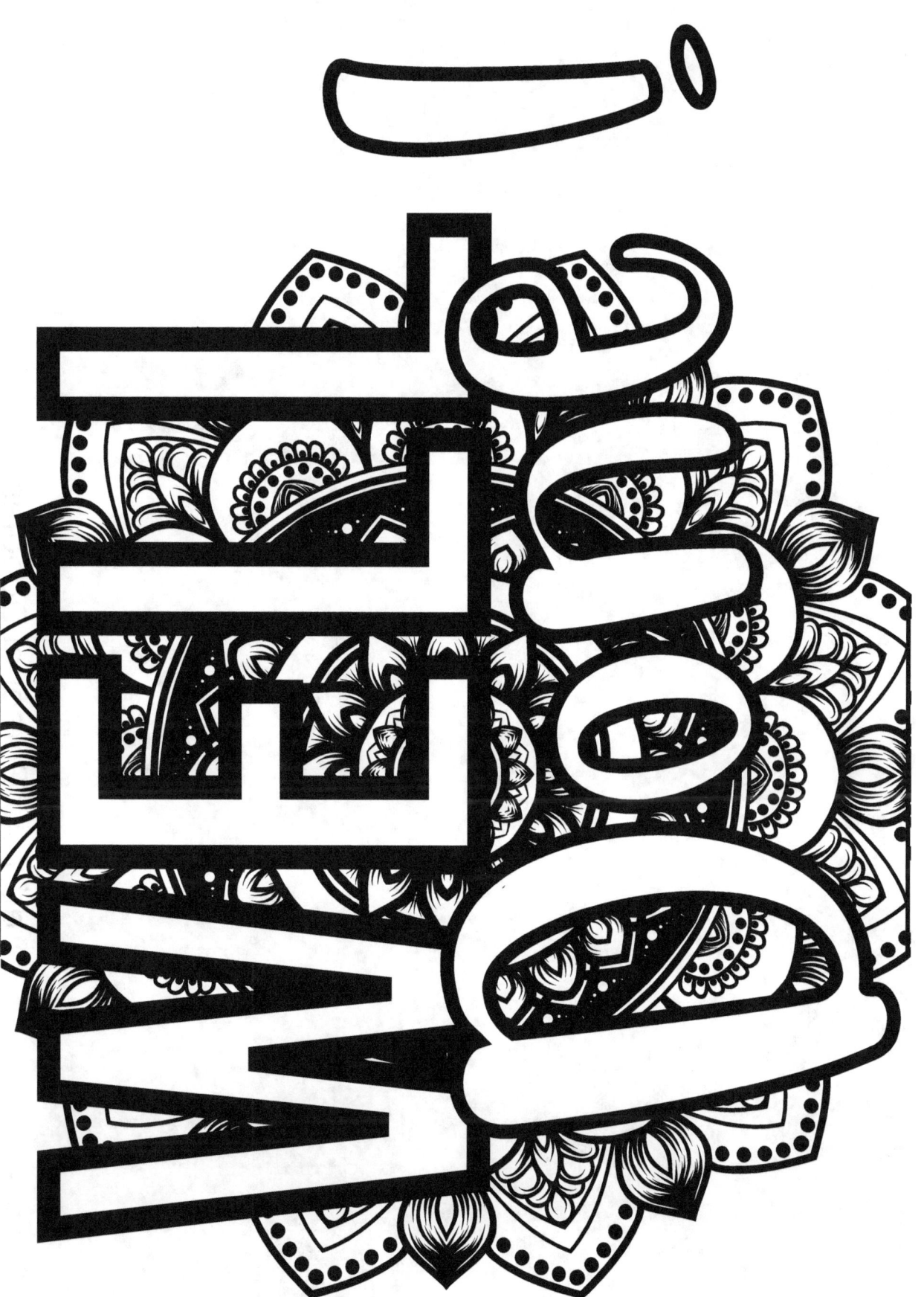

Add Your Personal Doodles

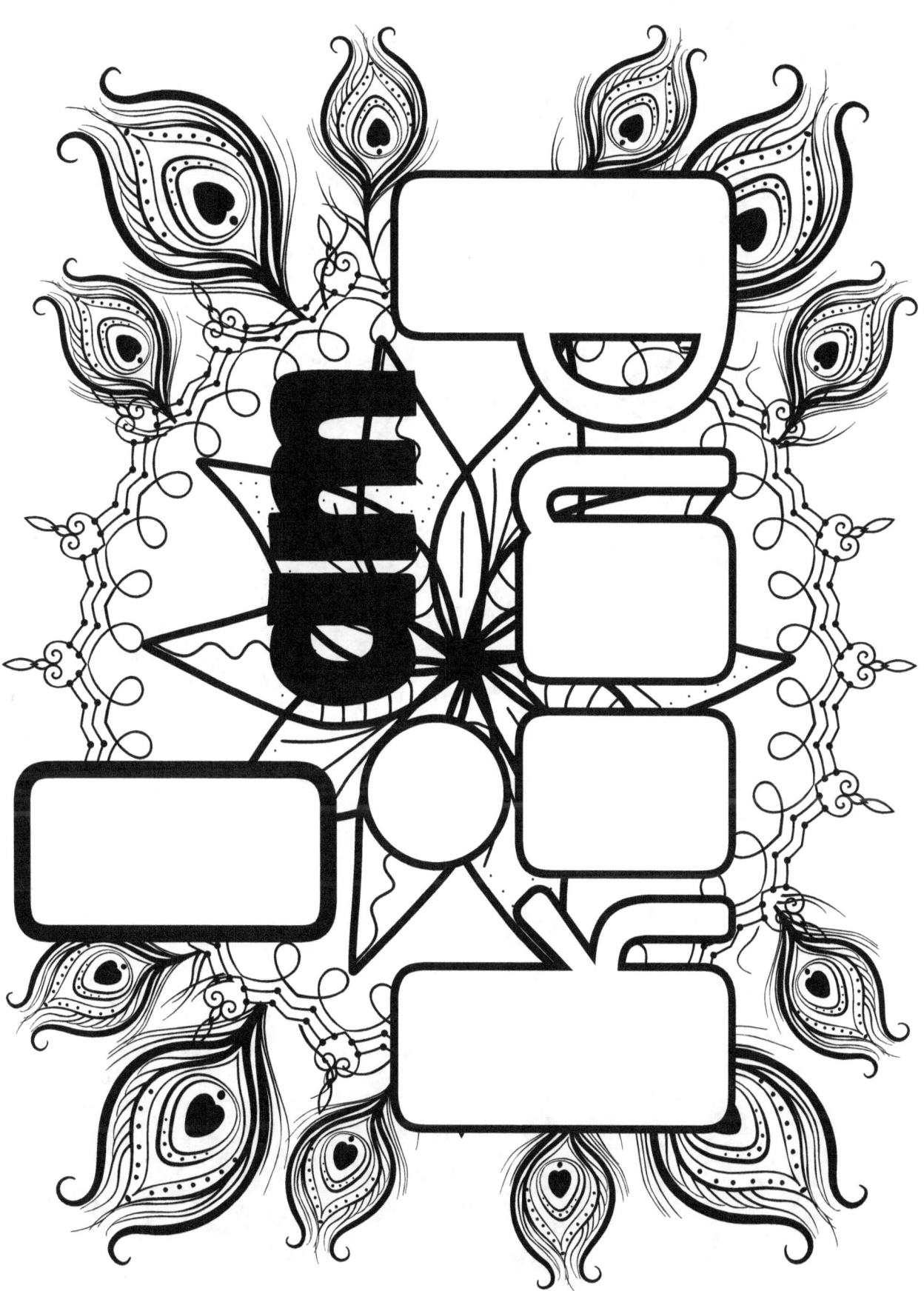

Add Your Personal Doodles

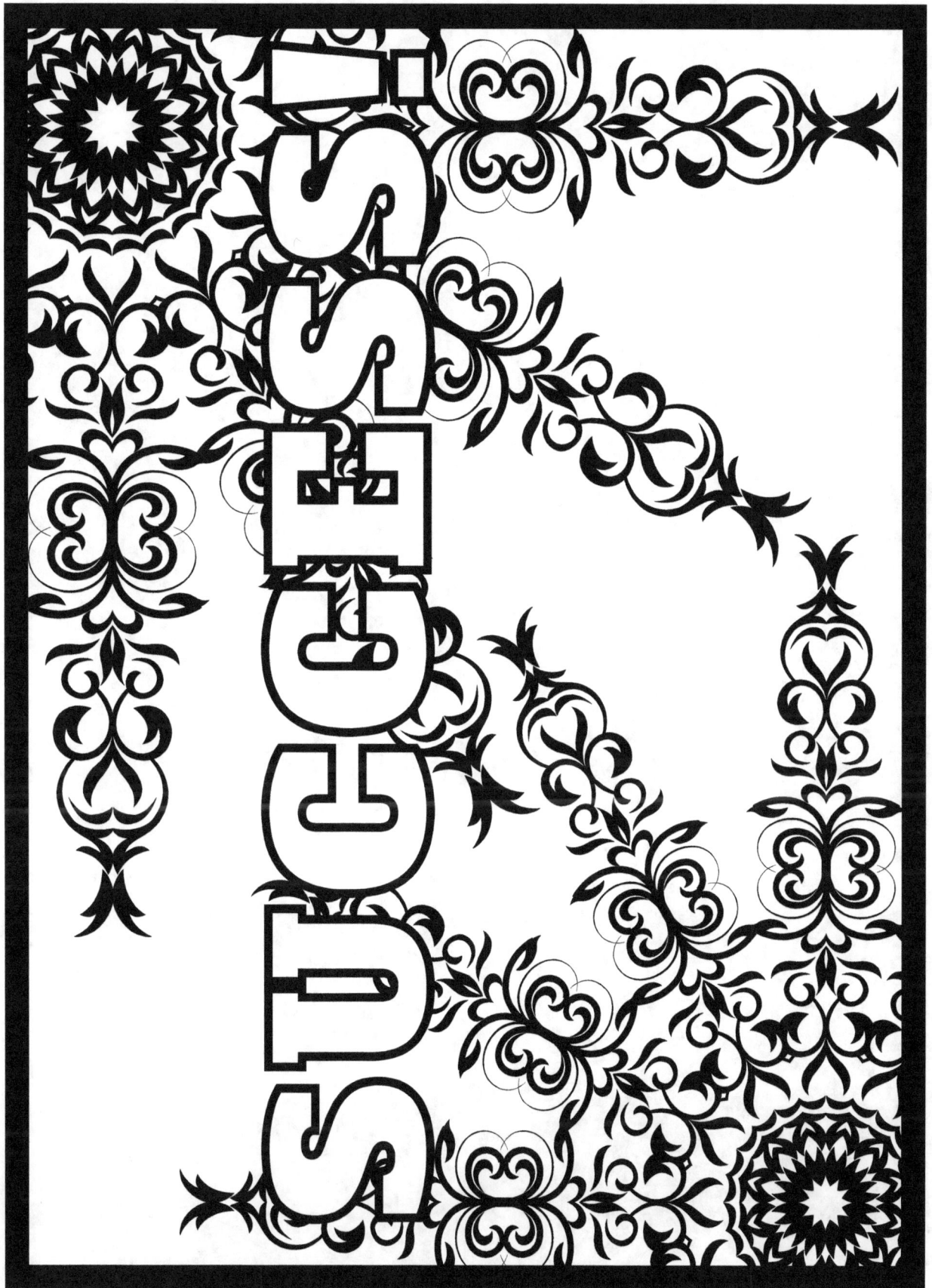

Add Your Personal Doodles

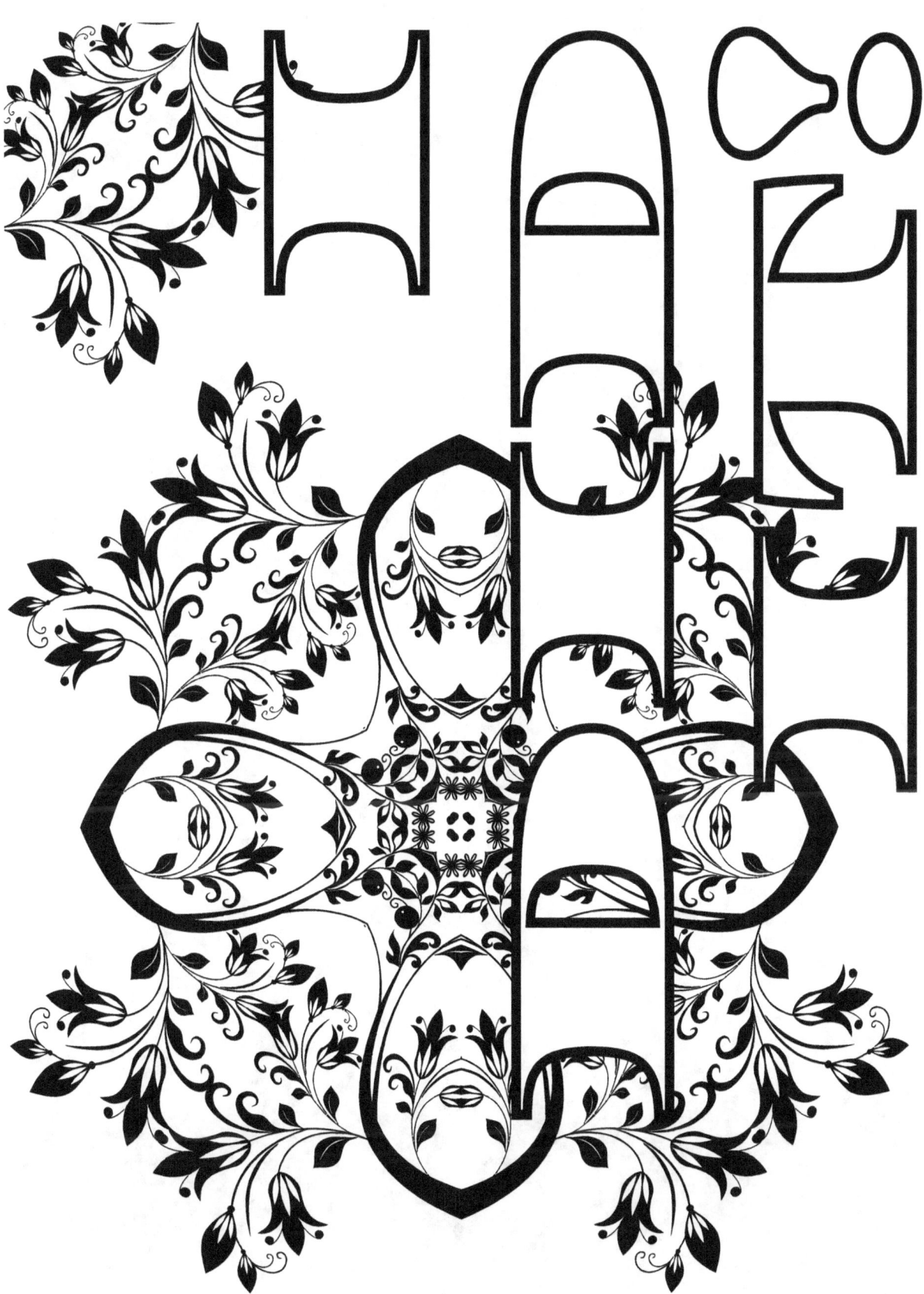

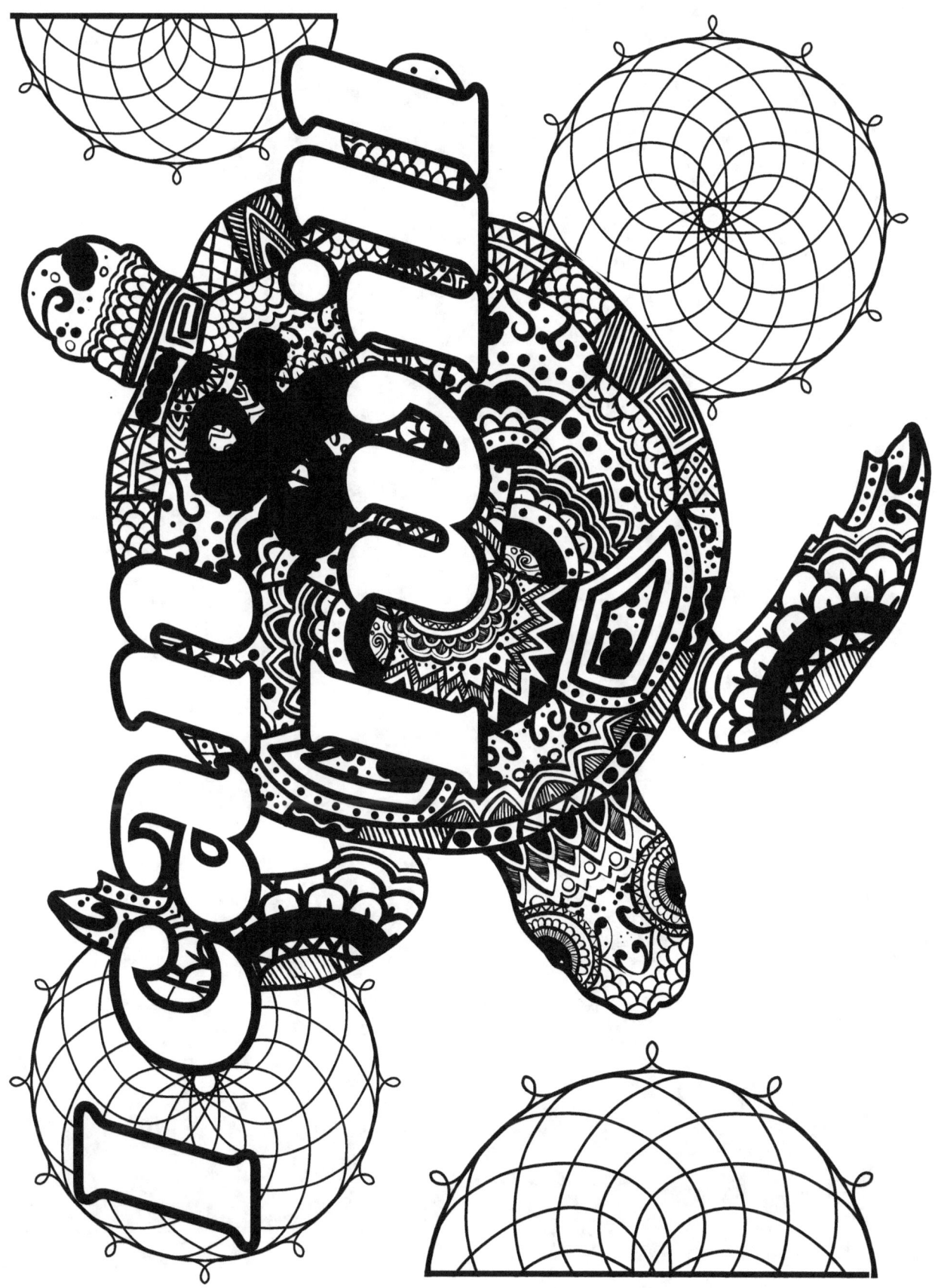

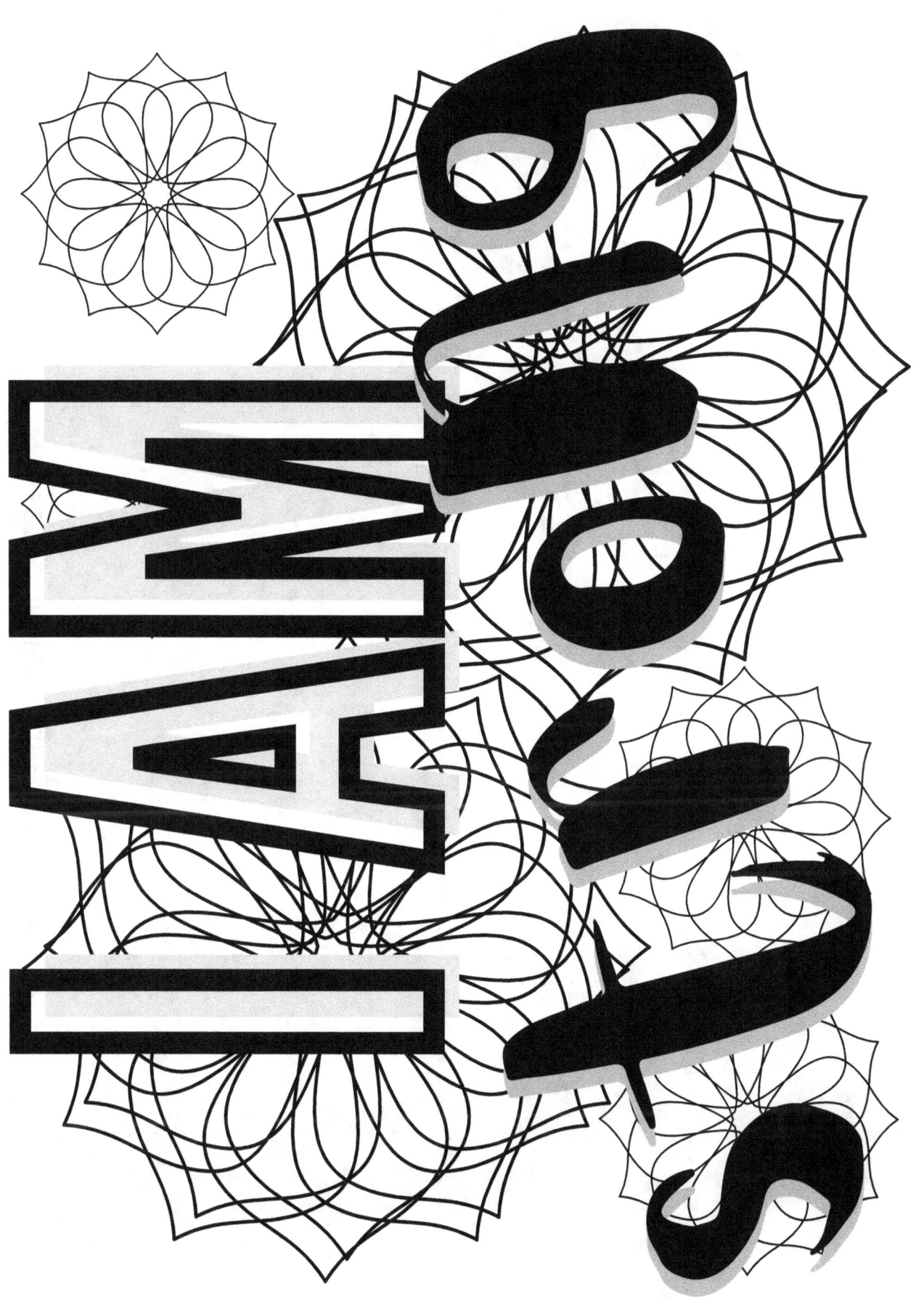

Add Your Personal Doodles

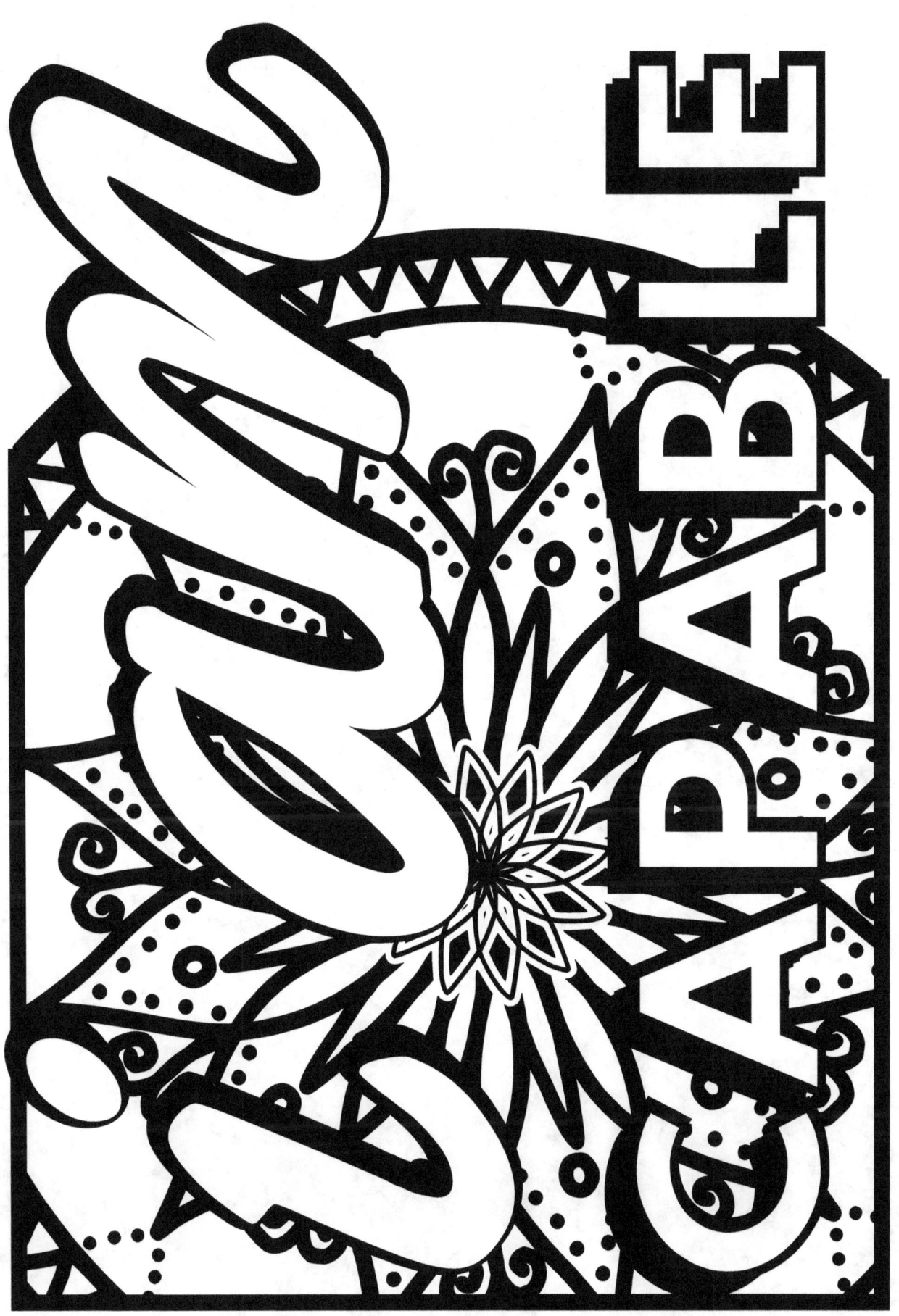

Add Your Personal Doodles

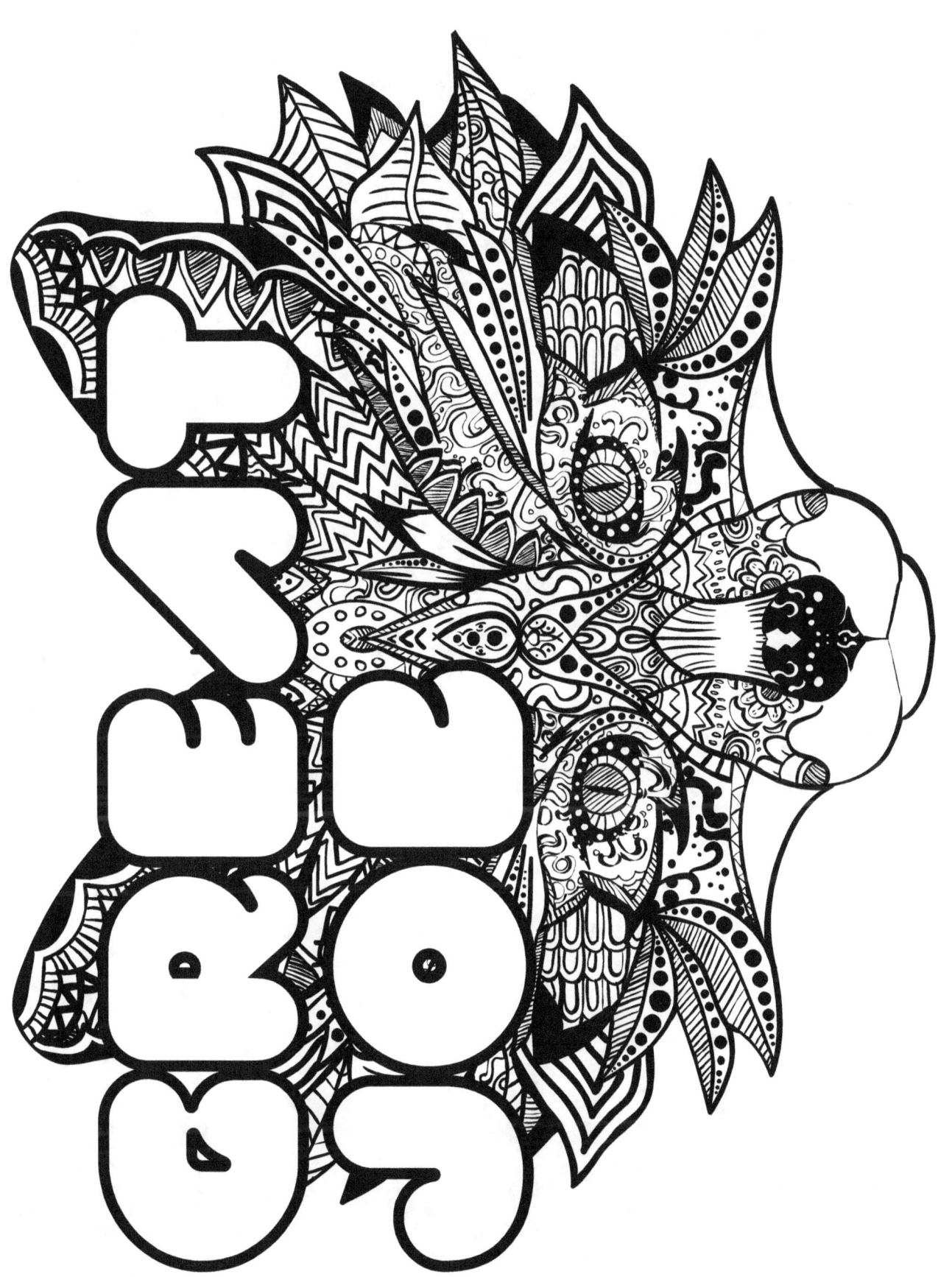

Add Your Personal Doodles

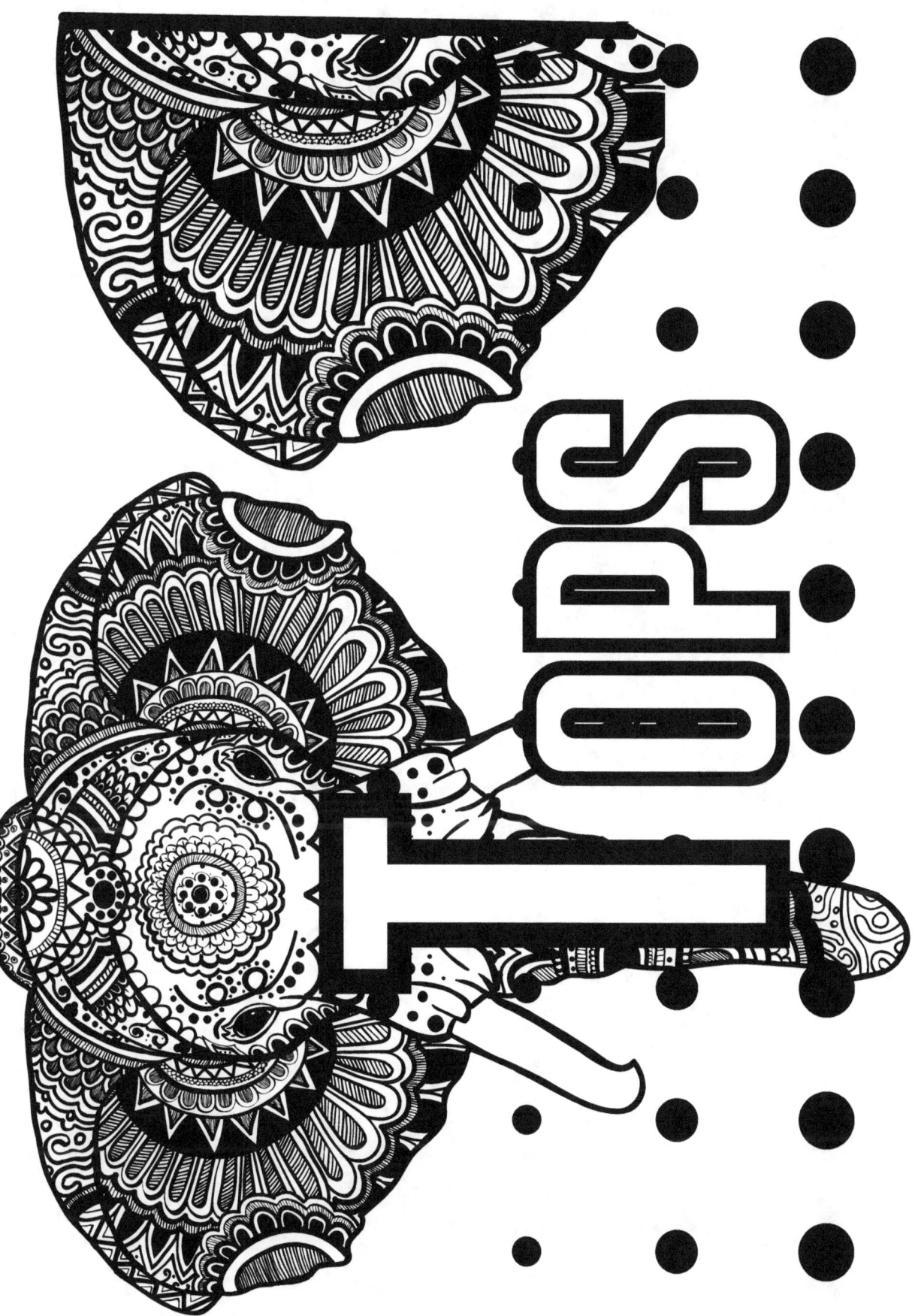

Add Your Personal Doodles

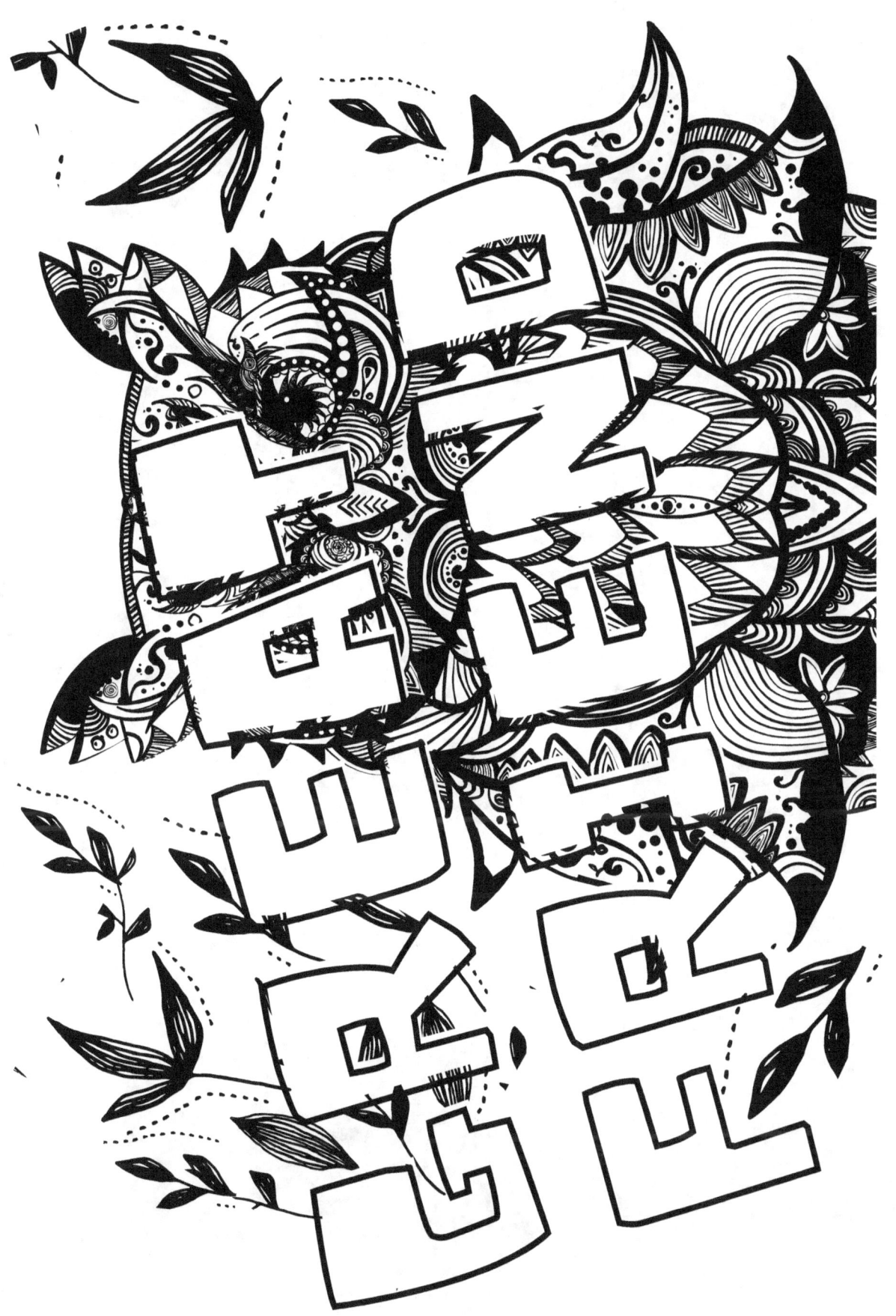

Add Your Personal Doodles

www.ingramcontent.com/pod-product-compliance
Lightning Source LLC
Chambersburg PA
CBHW080440220526
45465CB00009B/3372